WHY DO WE NEED RULES?

NANCY DICKMANN • ANDRÉS LANDAZÁBAL

WAYLAND

First published in Great Britain in 2021
by Wayland
Copyright © Hodder and Stoughton, 2021

Editor: Sarah Peutrill
Designer: Clare Mills

HB ISBN: 978 1 5263 1031 6
PB ISBN: 978 1 5263 1032 3

Printed and bound in Dubai
Wayland, an imprint of
Hachette Children's Group
Part of Hodder and Stoughton
Carmelite House
50 Victoria Embankment
London EC4Y 0DZ
An Hachette UK Company
www.hachette.co.uk
www.hachettechildrens.co.uk

Contents

What if there were no rules?

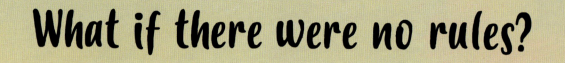

Sometimes it feels like there are rules about everything. Don't do this! Don't do that, either! Brush your teeth before bed! Wouldn't it be nice if you could just do whatever you want?

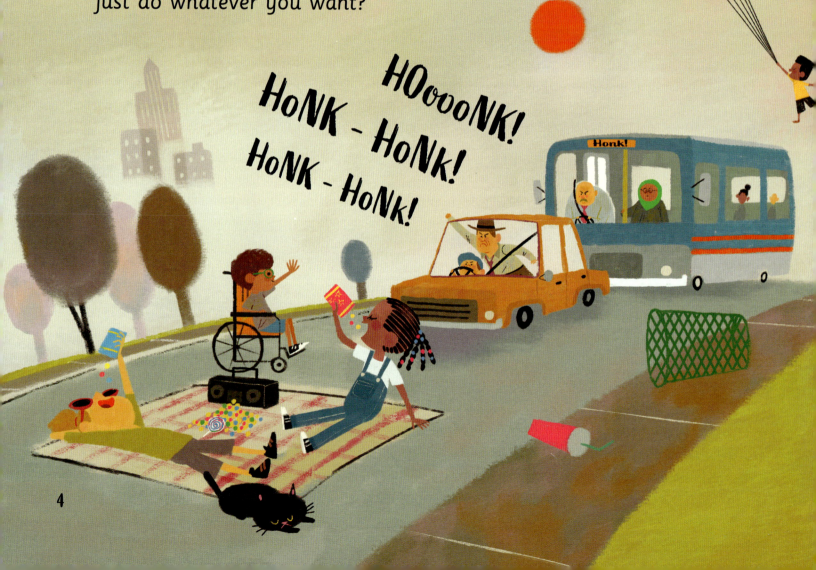

HOoooNK!

HoNK - HoNk!

HoNK - HoNK!

4

Now, imagine a world where there are no rules at all. Children can drive a car or fly a plane. People can take whatever they want, without paying. They won't get stopped or punished.

A world with no rules sounds like it would be fun. But rules are there for a reason. They help keep people safe. They help make sure that everyone is treated fairly.

Who makes the rules?

Okay, so it's clear that we do actually need rules.
Otherwise, it would be chaos!
But who makes the rules?

Teachers make rules for their classroom about sharing, working and tidying up.

Your parents probably make rules to follow at home.

Governments make laws.
Laws are another kind of rule.
A law might set a limit on
how fast people can drive.

Do I have a say?

Usually, the people in charge make the rules. But at home
or school, you might help decide on the rules. Most people
don't make laws themselves. But adults can vote for the
people they think will do the best job at making laws.

Why should I follow the rules?

Once you've made your rules, they will only work
if everyone agrees to follow them. Why do people
sometimes decide to break the rules?

Would you follow a rule that said you had to tidy your room
before you can play? You might be tempted to break it.
Playing outside is more fun!

What about a rule that said you had to wear your pants on your head? You'd probably be tempted to break this one too. You'd look really silly, and breaking the rule doesn't harm anyone.

The pants rule is silly. Good rules aren't. But would you still follow them if you saw other people breaking them?

How do we make rules fair?

The people who make rules must think carefully about how they will affect people. Do they treat everyone fairly?

What if there was a rule that only right-handed people are allowed to eat ice cream? If you are right-handed, you might be happy. But what about if you are left-handed? The rule is unfair to you.

Can we change the rules?

Sometimes a rule might be good for some people, but bad for others. You may not want to follow it. Some people try to change rules or laws that they think are unfair. They might write letters or stage protests.

Can you think of any rules that are unfair?
What can you do about them?

11

What if we don't agree?

Charlie and Aruna are best friends. They both want to buy the same magic set with their pocket money, but there is only one left in the shop. Who should have it?

The two friends stand there arguing. In fact, they are so busy arguing that they don't notice Sienna buying it for herself!

Charlie and Aruna both lost out because they weren't willing
to compromise. This means giving up part of what you want.
They could have agreed to split the cost and share the magic set.
Then they both could have enjoyed it, even if they had to share.

Have you ever had to compromise?

Can we all work together?

No matter whether a problem is big or small, solving it often takes compromise.

Ameera's class is holding a sports day, and her classmates have some pretty crazy ideas about what sports to include. Jake wants an egg and spoon race. Flora is desperate for a camel-riding race. Olivia wants pole-vaulting and Ali suggests skydiving! Their teacher just wants everyone to survive and not break anything.

14

The class will have to compromise to make it work. Even countries sometimes compromise! The United Nations is a group of many different countries. They try to stop wars and make sure that everyone is treated fairly. Each country doesn't always get what it wants. But they work together to solve problems.

Is everyone equal?

Some laws are really useful. They make sure that people are treated fairly. In most places, everyone has the same rights. They can go to school. They can see a doctor when they are ill. They have the right to be protected by the police.

But there is no rule that says everyone has to be exactly the same. It would be really boring if there were! We wear different clothes and have different jobs and hobbies. This all seems perfectly fair.

There are other differences, too. Some people are rich. Others are poor. These differences feel less fair. But they are not against the law. Do you think that they should be?

Does anyone deserve to be rich?

Many people would like to be rich, but only the lucky few have a lot of money. They might get it by:

- having it passed down through their family

- starting a business and making it successful

- being really good at football, acting or music.

Not many people have the talent to be a top footballer. They are paid a lot. Doctors are paid well, too. Their job takes many years of training.

Firefighters risk their lives to save people. Nurses care for the sick. Both these jobs are really important, but neither will make you rich. Do you think this is fair?

How should we decide which jobs get the best pay?
Or should all jobs be paid the same?

Can I say whatever I want?

Not many things in life are free. But speech is! In most countries there are laws to protect your right to speak out. You can't be punished for giving your opinion.

But even if you can say what you like, does that mean you should? Telling your friend that his cool dance moves make him look like a clumsy elephant won't break the law. But it will hurt his feelings.

Are there limits to free speech?

There are a few things that you can't say. You're not allowed to spread lies that will hurt a person. You can't encourage others to break the law. And a business can't lie in its advertising. If they claim that eating their pasta sauce will give you the power to fly, they'll be in trouble!

Do I have a duty to help others?

There are many things you can do to help others, or to make your community better. Here are just a few:

- picking up litter

- donating old toys or raising money for charity

- planting trees

- helping the elderly.

Helping out in your community is a choice. You don't have to do it. But many people want to do their part. They know that if they are ever in need, their community will help them.

Who helps me?

People are always there to help you. For some, like ambulance drivers, it's their job. Others, like sports coaches, often don't get paid. They love what they do and want to help others. Think about people who help you. How many can you name?

WICKLOW COUNTY COUNCIL
LIBRARY SERVICE

Do animals have rights too?

If dogs and cats were in charge, what rules would they make? Unlimited treats? Five walks a day? How about all sunny patches being reserved for cats only? Maybe it's a good thing that animals don't make rules!

Humans make laws, and some of them protect pets and wild animals. But we still kill animals to eat them. We lock them in zoos for people to look at.

Animals don't have rights like we do. If they did, the world would look very different.

- Everyone would be vegan.
- There would be no more zoos.
- Working animals would get paid.
- Animals couldn't be sold at pet shops.

What rights do you think animals should have?

Can rules help protect the planet?

Earth is amazing. And it's the only home we've got!
Our planet provides everything we need to survive.
In return, we should protect it ... right?

There are easy ways to help. We can recycle our waste.
We can plant trees. We can walk or cycle instead of driving.
If you're the only one doing these things, it won't make
much of a difference. But what if everyone pitched in?

Making laws is one way to make sure that everyone does their part. There are already some laws that protect the planet. They might ban plastic bags or straws. They might set aside land for nature reserves.

Can you think of any other laws that would save the planet?

27

Do rules make things better?

In a world with no rules people could do anything they wanted, even if it was unsafe or unfair. No one would stop you from riding your bike down the stairs. And no one would stop someone from stealing your toys.

But would we really act that way? Would people keep doing the right thing, even if there were no rules? Would you?

A world with rules can be just as bad, if the rules aren't good. Bad rules treat people unfairly. They take away people's rights. People work to change these rules.

What do you think? Are rules good or bad?

Glossary

advertising — images, messages or videos that encourage people to buy a particular product or service

ban — to make it against the law to make, sell, use or do something

compromise — to give up part of what you want in order to settle a disagreement

donating — giving away money or things to a good cause, without expecting anything in return

free speech — the idea that governments can't control what you are allowed to say

law — a rule made by a government, which people must follow

nature reserve — land set aside and looked after so that plants and animals can thrive there

protest — an organised demonstration where people can show what they think about a particular issue

rights — things or freedoms that people are entitled to have

United Nations — a worldwide group of countries that work together to solve problems and settle disputes

vegan — a person who does not eat any food from animals or use products made from animals

vote — to show who you think should be elected, or which choice you prefer, usually by making a mark on a piece of paper

wild animals — animals that are not kept by farmers, in zoos or as pets

What is philosophy?

Philosophy is a word that means 'a love of wisdom'. It's a way of trying to understand the world by asking questions. Philosophers also try to understand people, and why we act the way we do. That's what you've been doing as you read this book!

Philosophers have been asking questions since ancient times, and there are still philosophers today. They don't always find a clear answer to their questions. But they keep thinking! Many of their questions lead to even more questions.

You can be a philosopher, too. You just need to be curious about yourself, and about the world around you. Think about tricky questions and discuss them with your friends. For example, you could talk about whether a rule is fair or not. Do you all think the same? What can you learn from your friends' ideas?

Index